YOU BE THE JURY
Courtroom IV

Marvin Miller

Illustrated by Bob Roper

SCHOLASTIC INC.
New York Toronto London Auckland Sydney

Also by Marvin Miller:

YOU BE THE JURY
YOU BE THE JURY: COURTROOM II
YOU BE THE JURY: COURTROOM III
YOU BE THE DETECTIVE
WHO DUNNIT?

. . for Robby, again . . . .

ISBN 0-590-44380-1

12 11 10 9 8 7 6 5 4 3 2 1   1 2 3 4 5 6/9

Printed in the U.S.A.   28

First Scholastic printing, September 1991

CONTENTS

Order in the Court

LADIES AND GENTLEMEN OF THE JURY:
This court is now in session. My name is Judge John Dennenberg. You are the jury, and the trials are set to begin.

You have a serious responsibility. Will the innocent be sent to jail and the guilty go free? Let's hope not. Your job is to make sure that justice is served.

Read each case carefully. Study the evidence presented and then decide.

GUILTY OR NOT GUILTY??

Both sides of the case will be presented to you. The person who has the complaint is called the *plaintiff*. He or she has brought the case to court. If a crime is involved, the State is the accuser.

The person being accused is called the *defendant*. The defendant is pleading his or her innocence

1

and presents a much different version of what happened.

IN EACH CASE, THREE PIECES OF EVIDENCE WILL BE PRESENTED AS EXHIBITS A, B, AND C. EXAMINE THE EXHIBITS VERY CAREFULLY. A *CLUE* TO THE SOLUTION OF EACH CASE WILL BE FOUND THERE. IT WILL DIRECTLY POINT TO THE INNOCENCE OR GUILT OF THE ACCUSED.

Remember, each side will try to convince you that his or her version is what actually happened. BUT YOU MUST MAKE THE FINAL DECISION.

The Case of the Unhappy Hunter

LADIES AND GENTLEMEN OF THE JURY:

If a person is injured on someone else's land, the property owner is responsible. But if people are warned to stay away, the owner is not liable.

This is the point of law you must consider today.

Brendan Mosby, the plaintiff, is suing Hector Peebles for failing to warn hunters that there were dangerous animal traps on his land. Mr. Peebles, the defendant, says that he had posted warning signs to keep people away.

On January 4, Brendan Mosby skipped work to go hunting in Mountain Lakes. The area is located 20 miles outside of Bedford. Each year, hundreds of persons go there to hunt pheasants.

Despite a full day in Mountain Lakes, Mosby was disappointed. He failed to hunt down a single bird.

Mr. Mosby explained to the court how he entered Hector Peebles's property:

"I'd been hunting all day. Early in the afternoon it began snowing real hard. I was growing tired. After hunting for hours, I had hardly seen any pheasants. I was disgusted and decided to go home.

"When I started walking back to my car, I couldn't find the main road. Suddenly I realized I was lost. I got a little scared.

"I must have roamed through Mountain Lakes for over an hour. Finally it stopped snowing. I spotted some telephone poles in the distance. I figured I must be near the main road."

Mosby headed for the road, but he did not realize he was walking through the private property owned by Hector Peebles.

The plaintiff enters as EXHIBIT A a diagram of his location. Peebles's land is in the shaded area.

Mr. Mosby was asked to describe his accident. First the question and then his answer:

Q: Didn't you know you were trespassing on Peebles's land?

A: How could I? There were no signs. I just figured I was walking through the Mountain Lakes hunting area.

Q: Will you tell the court how you were injured?

A: I saw the telephone poles in the distance and headed in their direction. I walked through what I thought was a snow-covered path. Suddenly I felt something sharp clamp tightly around my left leg. It cut into it, and I fell to the ground. Blood started seeping through my pants leg. The pain was terrible.

Q: How did you manage to free yourself?

A: I was really dazed by the pain. But I had enough strength to pry open the jaws of the trap around my leg.

Q: Did you see any signs on the property that warned of animal traps?

A: No. Definitely not. There were no signs on the land.

Brendan Mosby is suing Hector Peebles for medical expenses from his injury and for the pain and suffering it caused. He says that if the land had been properly marked, he never would have walked into the trap.

Mr. Peebles claims that the plaintiff was mistaken. He had posted warning signs all over his property. Brendan Mosby should have seen them.

Peebles testified as follows:

"When I bought the land twelve years ago, the first thing I did was build a wire fence around it. It kept out hunters. And most of all, I didn't want any animals ruining my garden.

"But sometimes an animal would break through my fence, so I put in traps to catch them.

"I check the fence regularly. The afternoon of Mosby's accident, I saw that a section of my fence was down. I would have fixed it then and there, but it started to snow real hard. I thought it could wait until the following day."

Mr. Peebles entered as EXHIBIT B a photo of the broken fence. The footprints show where Brendan Mosby entered Peebles's property.

"If Mosby had been careful, he would have seen my sign. It warns trespassers of my animal traps. I post signs near every trap."

After Mosby was injured, Peebles took a photograph of the area. This is entered as EXHIBIT C. It shows the trap and the warning sign on a nearby tree.

Mr. Peebles continued his testimony:

"I can't be responsible for Mosby's accident. There was enough daylight for him to see my sign. Brendan Mosby walked on my property — plain and simple. He was too lazy to walk around it to reach the main road.

"Mosby never should have been on my land. It was his own carelessness that caused the accident."

LADIES AND GENTLEMEN OF THE JURY:

You have just heard the Case of the Unhappy Hunter. You must decide the merits of Brendan Mosby's claim.

Is Hector Peebles responsible for Mosby's injury? Or should the hunter have seen the warning sign?

6

EXHIBIT A

MAIN ROAD

LAKE

HECTOR PEEBLE'S
LAND

MOUNTAIN

EXHIBIT C

VERDICT

HECTOR PEEBLES IS RESPONSIBLE.

Peebles put up the sign after the accident occurred.

The place where Mosby was injured is shown in EXHIBIT C. The tree limbs are covered with snow. But there is no snow on top of the warning sign. Peebles must have nailed it to the tree *after* it stopped snowing.

The Case of the Exploding Tire

LADIES AND GENTLEMEN OF THE JURY:

When a person buys a product, often she or he is given a written warranty. This guarantees that the product is of good quality.

Sometimes a warranty is written to limit the seller's responsibility. This is called a *limited warranty*. It describes exactly what the seller will do if the product is faulty.

Molly Kramer, the plaintiff, is in court today and claims her car was damaged because of a tire she bought from Ernie's Tire and Auto Center.

Ernie Walker, the defendant, agrees to replace the tire. But he refuses to pay for anything else.

Molly Kramer explained to the court how the damage occurred:

"I own a fifteen-year-old Penza. It's a great car, but the front tires were worn pretty badly. And replacement tires are so expensive these days. When I heard about a tire sale at Ernie's, I drove right over.

"The sale seemed like a bargain, so I bought two new ones. It must have taken about a half hour to replace both tires. I had some work done on my engine, too.

"About a week later, while I was driving home from work, I heard a loud bang. My car jerked to the side of the road. It was really scary."

Miss Kramer got out of her car and inspected the front end. Her new right tire was a rubbery blob.

The new tire had exploded, and the car's front fender was blown partly off. She phoned Ernie Walker and had him tow her car to his garage.

The plaintiff is suing Ernie Walker to replace the tire. She also wants him to pay for the cost of a new front fender.

Molly Kramer continued her testimony:

"When I demanded that Ernie pay for all costs, he refused. He said that he was responsible only for replacing the blown-out tire. I would have to pay for the fender myself.

"Ernie showed me a copy of the bill with a tire warranty printed on the bottom. But I never saw the bill before. It had my signature on it. Ernie must have faked it.

"He must have copied my name on the bill from my signature on the check I gave him."

Molly Kramer's check was entered as EXHIBIT A.

Ernie Walker told his side of the story to the court:

"I warned Miss Kramer that her car was in bad shape and that the wheels needed to be aligned. I tried to convince the lady to get it fixed.

"When she refused, I pointed out the limited warranty to Miss Kramer and had her sign the bill. I gave her a copy to keep."

EXHIBIT B is Ernie Walker's copy of the bill with the tire warranty that has Molly Kramer's signature. Note the wording of the limited warranty.

The defendant claims that his only responsibility is to replace Molly Kramer's tire. He refuses to pay for anything else and says she should contact the tire manufacturer if she isn't satisfied.

A garage worker, Chester Snibbe, saw Ernie give the warranty to Molly Kramer. He took the stand to testify.

Under questioning, Chester said he remembered the woman's visit very clearly:

Q: Where were you when Ernie Walker gave the warranty to the plaintiff?
A: I was replacing a bulb inside the lady's car. Miss Kramer and Ernie were standing in the repair area by the desk.
Q: Did you actually see Ernie hand her the warranty?
A: Sure I did. I was in the front seat fixing the bulb. Ernie had been working under the hood,

adjusting the engine. He kept the motor running so he could keep an eye on things in case something went wrong. I saw Ernie fill out the warranty bill and then saw Miss Kramer sign it.

Q: Are you certain?

A: Sure, I'm certain. The warranty forms are on Ernie's desk in the repair area. After she signed it, Ernie kept the white copy and gave a yellow one to Miss Kramer. She put it in her purse.

Q: Did she ask Ernie any questions about the warranty?

A: Not that I know of. Ernie was still checking the engine when I left. I don't know what they talked about.

Q: Did the garage have any signs posted, warning customers of the limited warranty?

A: Sure. There is a sign near the desk in the repair area.

EXHIBIT C is the repair area in Ernie's garage. It shows where the notice is posted on the wall. Questioning of Chester Snibbe continued:

Q: Look at the door next to the sign. Is it possible the door was open and covered the notice?

A: I don't remember. I think the door was closed. But anyway, I saw Miss Kramer sign the warranty. I think that should be good enough.

14

*　　*　　*

LADIES AND GENTLEMEN OF THE JURY:
You have just heard the Case of the Exploding Tire. You must decide the merits of the plaintiff's claim. Be sure to carefully examine the evidence in EXHIBITS A, B, and C.

Was Molly Kramer given a limited warranty? Or was the testimony against her a lie?

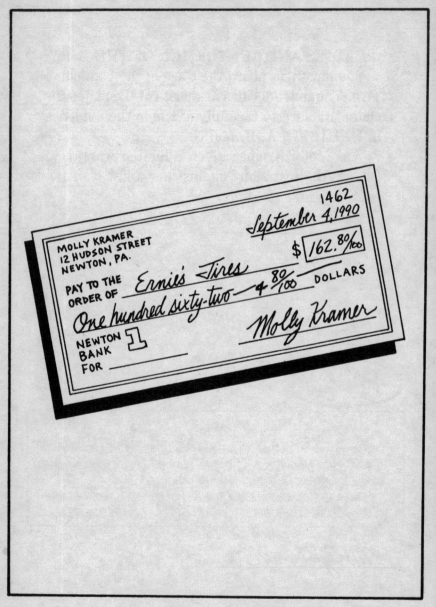

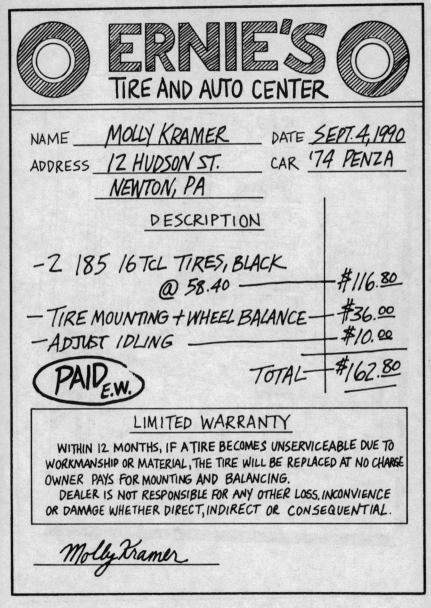

ERNIE'S
TIRE AND AUTO CENTER

NAME _MOLLY KRAMER_   DATE _SEPT. 4, 1990_
ADDRESS _12 HUDSON ST._   CAR _'74 PENZA_
NEWTON, PA

DESCRIPTION

- 2 185 16 TCL TIRES, BLACK
  @ 58.40 ————————————— $116.80
- TIRE MOUNTING + WHEEL BALANCE —— $36.00
- ADJUST IDLING ————————— $10.00

PAID E.W.   TOTAL —— $162.80

LIMITED WARRANTY

WITHIN 12 MONTHS, IF A TIRE BECOMES UNSERVICEABLE DUE TO
WORKMANSHIP OR MATERIAL, THE TIRE WILL BE REPLACED AT NO CHARGE
OWNER PAYS FOR MOUNTING AND BALANCING.
   DEALER IS NOT RESPONSIBLE FOR ANY OTHER LOSS, INCONVIENCE
OR DAMAGE WHETHER DIRECT, INDIRECT OR CONSEQUENTIAL.

Molly Kramer

EXHIBIT C

VERDICT

THE TESTIMONY WAS A LIE.

EXHIBIT C shows the desk where Chester Snibbe claimed Ernie and Miss Kramer were standing. While it was being repaired, Miss Kramer's car would have been parked in *front* of the desk.

Chester never could have seen Molly Kramer at the desk, signing the warranty. He was sitting in the front seat of her car, but the hood of the car was *up*, blocking his view. All Chester could have seen was the car hood.

The Case of the Counterfeit Shopper

LADIES AND GENTLEMEN OF THE JURY:
Distributing fake money is a criminal offense. It is punishable by a long jail sentence.

The federal government, represented by the district attorney, has charged Gilbert Nelson with buying merchandise using counterfeit money.

Mr. Nelson, the defendant, claims he is innocent. He says that it was another shopper who passed the counterfeit bills.

A security guard for Appleby's Department Store was called to the stand:

"My name is Jed Archer, and I have been a security guard with Appleby's for twenty-four years.

"I was at my station on the second floor when Rhonda, the cashier in the coat department, frantically waved in my direction.

"She showed me seven $10 bills that a customer had just given her. He had used them to buy a raincoat. She said the bills seemed funny.

"I examined them closely. They were all brand-new and looked real. But when I ran my thumb across their faces, they just didn't feel right."

EXHIBIT A is a close-up photograph of one of the $10 bills. A crime laboratory has identified it as counterfeit. Note how it compares with a genuine $10 bill. Lines on the outer margin and scroll of the fake bill are blurred and uneven.

Mr. Archer continued his testimony:

"Rhonda pointed across the floor at the man who had just given her the money. He was walking toward the down escalator. I yelled for him to stop. When he heard my voice, the man broke through the crowd and began to run.

"Appleby's Department Store has a steep escalator leading from the second floor to the main floor below. I had to think fast. I pushed the escalator button and switched the stairs so they moved upwards, in the opposite direction.

"Switching the direction of the escalator was a great idea. But the shopper was too quick. He ran down the steps faster than the escalator steps moved up. I chased, but couldn't catch him.

"By the time I was halfway down the steps, the counterfeiter had reached the main floor. He darted out the front door."

The security guard stopped the escalator and telephoned the police.

When officers arrived, they examined the area. A man's wallet was discovered on an escalator step.

EXHIBIT B shows where the wallet was found. An "X" marks the spot. The police believe it was dropped by the criminal during his escape.

Credit cards inside the wallet identified its owner. The wallet belonged to Gilbert Nelson. On this basis, Nelson was arrested. He is charged here today with passing counterfeit money.

Mr. Nelson states that the wallet is his, but he was not involved in the crime. He testified as follows:

"I'm innocent! Sure, I was shopping in Appleby's Department Store that afternoon. But I was nowhere near the coat department.

"There was a lot of yelling going on, and I saw it all happening. I heard the guard shout and run down the escalator. In fact, everyone in the store stopped to see what was going on."

Gilbert Nelson was questioned by the district attorney:

Q: How did your wallet get on the escalator steps?

A: It must have fallen out of my back pocket when I walked down the escalator. But that was after the counterfeiter fled. I left the department store about ten minutes later.

Q: The security guard testified that he stopped the escalator after the criminal escaped. The steps weren't moving. Why didn't you take an elevator instead of walking down the escalator?

A: It might have been easier, but it would have been slower. I was in a hurry. There were long lines at the elevators.

Q: Exactly where were you shopping?

A: I was at the necktie counter on the second floor. I never went near the coat department.

Q: Then how do you account for the counterfeit $10 bills in your wallet?

A: They must have been given to me as change by the clerk at the necktie counter. I remember giving her a $50 bill. The tie cost $9.95. She gave me change of a nickel and four $10 bills.

EXHIBIT C is Gilbert Nelson's wallet, discovered on the escalator steps. The four $10 bills in it have been shown to be counterfeit.

Mr. Nelson's lawyer claims that the counterfeiter could have used fake bills at the necktie counter first, before shopping in the coat department.

These were the counterfeit bills that the necktie clerk took from her cash register and gave to Gilbert Nelson as change.

LADIES AND GENTLEMEN OF THE JURY: You have just heard the Case of the Counterfeit Shopper. You must decide the merits of the district attorney's accusation. Be sure to carefully examine the evidence in EXHIBITS A, B, and C.

Was Gilbert Nelson the man who passed the fake bills? Or was he mistaken for the counterfeiter?

EXHIBIT A

GENUINE BILL

COUNTERFEIT BILL

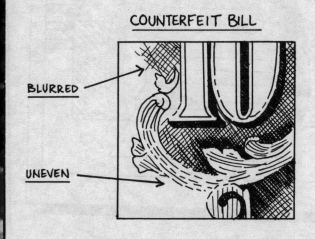

BLURRED

UNEVEN

EXHIBIT B

EXHIBIT C

VERDICT

GILBERT NELSON WAS INNOCENT.

While the counterfeiter was fleeing, the escalator was switched so the steps moved upwards.

If it had been the criminal's wallet that had dropped, the escalator would have carried it to the *top* step.

EXHIBIT B shows where Gilbert's wallet was found. It is on the *bottom* step of the escalator. This means Gilbert had walked down the steps after the counterfeiter had fled and the escalator was stopped.

The Case of the Newspaper Photograph

LADIES AND GENTLEMEN OF THE JURY:
If a newspaper reports that a person committed a crime and the article is false, the wronged person can sue. Printing inaccurate information is known as *libel*.

Glen Baxter, the plaintiff, accuses the *Daily Blaze* of falsely printing a news story that said he was arrested for robbery.

Lawyers for the *Daily Blaze* argue that the newspaper should not be blamed for the wrong information.

Mr. Baxter, a shoe store owner, testified as follows:

"Glen Baxter is my name, and I'm very, very upset. Let me tell you how this whole mix-up started.

"I was standing outside my store on Tilgman Street when I heard a woman scream that her purse had been stolen. I turned around and saw her point at a man. He was running the other way.

"I quickly ran after the thief and chased him down the street."

Baxter gained on the suspect. With one swift spurt, he lunged at the thief and wrestled him to the ground.

"After I tackled him, I held his hands tightly behind his back. A large crowd gathered, and I shouted for someone to call the police."

A nearby police car answered the call. A policeman broke through the crowd and arrested the thief. As Mr. Baxter handed him over, a flash went off at the rear of the crowd. A reporter for the *Daily Blaze* had taken a picture of the arrest.

Glen Baxter continued his testimony:

"Other policemen arrived. I didn't want to be involved. As soon as the purse snatcher was arrested, I quickly slipped into the crowd."

The next day, when the plaintiff read a report of the robbery in the *Daily Blaze*, he was shocked to see a picture of himself standing with the thief and the arresting policeman. But the caption under the picture wrongly identified Glen Baxter as the purse snatcher.

EXHIBIT A is the newspaper article that reported the arrest. Baxter, wearing a white shirt, is described as the thief.

Mr. Baxter claims that the *Daily Blaze*'s mistake caused a loss of business for his shoe store.

"I moved to this town about a year ago. After

I bought the store, business started to improve. But when the picture appeared, customers started avoiding me. They began shopping at another shoe store downtown."

Glen Baxter is suing the *Daily Blaze* for his lost business and for damaging his reputation. Even though the newspaper printed a correction, many people never read it. They still think of him as a thief.

Walter Tubb, a reporter for the *Daily Blaze*, took the stand.

"This is all a terrible mistake. I was the one who took the picture. But it was a policeman who gave me the wrong information. The police are the ones to blame, not my newspaper."

Mr. Tubb testified as follows. First the question and then his answer:

Q: Did you write the caption under the picture?
A: Sure, I admit to it. But I got the information from a policeman at the crime scene. I wrote the picture's caption from my notes.
Q: What did the policeman say?
A: He told me about the robbery and that the person standing on the arresting policeman's right had stolen a lady's purse. The other man on the policeman's left had caught him.

The thief was later identified as Harry Hooper.

He is a known criminal with a prior history of petty theft. Hooper's police record appears as EXHIBIT B.

Walter Tubb's questioning continued:

Q: Could you have been mistaken? Is it possible that in the confusion you wrote down the wrong information?

A: Absolutely not. I'm certain of it. I'm positive I was told that the robber was standing on the policeman's right.

Q: What was the name of the officer who gave you the information?

A: I don't know. With everything going on, I never had time to ask him. I don't think I'd recognize him.

Q: Didn't you see Mr. Baxter leave the crime scene and slip into the crowd after the arrest? Couldn't you have figured out he wasn't the thief?

A: I went back to my office right after I took the picture. I never saw Baxter leave.

Lawyers for the *Daily Blaze* presented EXHIBIT C, a page from Walter Tubb's notebook. It shows how he clearly marked the people in the photograph he had taken. He used these notes to write the caption under the picture.

The *Daily Blaze* argues that the Police Department is to blame. They say that the notes in

Walter Tubb's notebook were copied down directly from a policeman's statement.

Their newspaper has a reputation for being careful, not careless. They ask that the charges against the newspaper be dismissed.

LADIES AND GENTLEMEN OF THE JURY:
You have just heard the Case of the Newspaper Photograph. You must decide the merits of Glen Baxter's claim. Be sure to carefully examine the evidence in EXHIBITS A, B, and C.

Did a policeman give the *Daily Blaze* wrong information? Or was the newspaper at fault?

EXHIBIT C

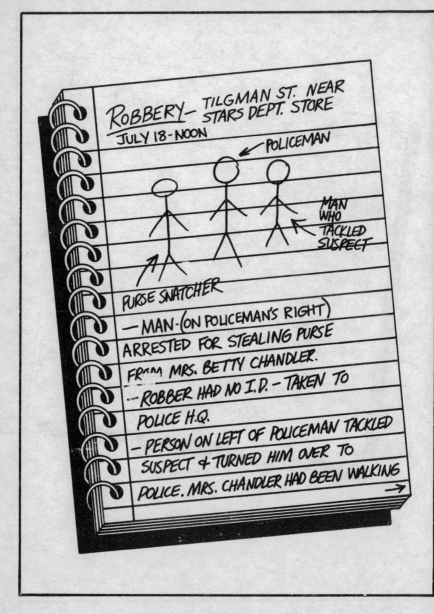

VERDICT

THE *DAILY BLAZE* WAS AT FAULT.

The window sign of Star's Department Store in EXHIBIT A has backward lettering. And the thief's scar is on his left cheek, while in EXHIBIT B it is on his right cheek. This means that the newspaper had printed the picture in *reverse*!

In developing the photograph, the negative was accidentally turned over. Everything in the picture was reversed. The person on the policeman's right was pictured on his left and vice versa.

When the reporter wrote the picture caption from his notes shown in EXHIBIT C, he didn't realize the mistake.

The Case of the Injured Inventor

LADIES AND GENTLEMEN OF THE JURY:

A person can buy an insurance policy that pays expenses if he or she becomes ill and unable to work. This is called *disability insurance*.

The person collects money so long as he or she is too sick to return to work.

Hubert Pickle is suing Writeall Insurance Company for refusing to pay him while he was recovering from an accident. He was bedridden for more than a month.

The insurance company accuses Mr. Pickle of pretending his injury was more serious than it actually was.

Hubert Pickle, the plaintiff, took the stand to explain how his accident occurred.

"Pickle is my name, and I'm president and owner of the Wonderwidgets Company. I invent things that people need but never imagined they could own.

"On July 18, I was testing my latest invention, an electric back scratcher. All of a sudden the machine went wild. It started pounding my back. It almost broke it."

Mr. Pickle claims his back was seriously hurt. He was confined to bed, hardly able to walk.

The attorney for Writeall Insurance questioned Mr. Pickle about his illness:

Q: How long were you confined to bed?

A: About six weeks. I'm asking the insurance company to pay me six weeks of disability insurance. They owe me $3,000.

Q: How did you care for yourself during this period?

A: I could barely get out of bed. My next-door neighbor visited me every morning. She would bring over my meals. She even arranged to move my bed downstairs so I could watch TV all day.

Q: Where is your Wonderwidgets Company located?

A: It's in my house. You see, I *am* the company. My laboratory is in the basement.

Q: Did you try to walk downstairs to your laboratory during the six weeks?

A: Sure I tried, but couldn't. I was eager to get back to work. I had just invented a nonstop waterfall that won a science award. I wanted to make a larger version to generate electricity. It's a solution to the energy crisis!

EXHIBIT A is this amazing waterfall. If you trace your finger along the water, you can see that it always flows downstream. The water can circulate forever.

The lawyer for the insurance company claims Hubert Pickle was faking the seriousness of his injury to collect insurance money. He says the inventor could have returned to his laboratory much earlier.

A private investigator, hired by Writeall, explained why the insurance company refuses to pay:

"My name is Walter Niff. I'm hired by Writeall Insurance Company whenever they think an injury is suspicious. They want me to find out if it's real or not.

"I was assigned to the Pickle case. He had taken out a disability policy with the company.

"I was sitting in my parked car, across the street from Hubert Pickle's house. His shades were pulled down. He even had shades on his basement windows. I watched his house for several hours.

"As I was about to leave, I saw smoke rising from the chimney on top of his house.

"I figured that Mr. Pickle had lit a fire in his fireplace. If he was strong enough to get out of bed, put some logs in the fireplace, and light them, he was able to go down to his laboratory."

When the investigator saw the smoke, he knocked

on Pickle's door. A voice answered. A few minutes later, Hubert Pickle opened the door.

The defense entered as EXHIBIT B a photograph of Pickle's living room as it appeared when Walter Niff was shown into the house.

The insurance investigator continued his testimony:

"Mr. Pickle looked like he was in a lot of pain. He said he barely had enough strength to get out of bed. He said he braced himself on the chair and struggled over to the door to open it for me.

"When I asked Mr. Pickle how he lit the fireplace, the inventor had an explanation. He had invented a remote control device that could light the fireplace while he was still in bed. He called it a Zaplighter.

"I asked Pickle to show me how it worked. He began fidgeting with the device. It was supposed to send an invisible current across the room. When it hit a log, it would start a fire.

"But when I checked the Zaplighter on another log, it wouldn't work. I even tried it up close. The invention was a fake. Hubert Pickle must have grabbed one of the gadgets around his house and pretended it was a Zaplighter."

The defense entered as EXHIBIT C a photograph of the remote control device. It shows the insurance investigator trying to light a log with the invention.

Writeall Insurance believes Hubert Pickle faked

his illness. He wasn't nearly as sick as he pretended to be. They claim he was well enough to walk over to the fireplace, put on some logs, and bend down to light them.

LADIES AND GENTLEMEN OF THE JURY: You have just heard the Case of the Injured Inventor. You must decide the merits of Hubert Pickle's claim. Be sure to carefully examine the evidence in EXHIBITS A, B, and C.

Should Hubert Pickle collect the full disability insurance? Or did he pretend to be sicker than he really was?

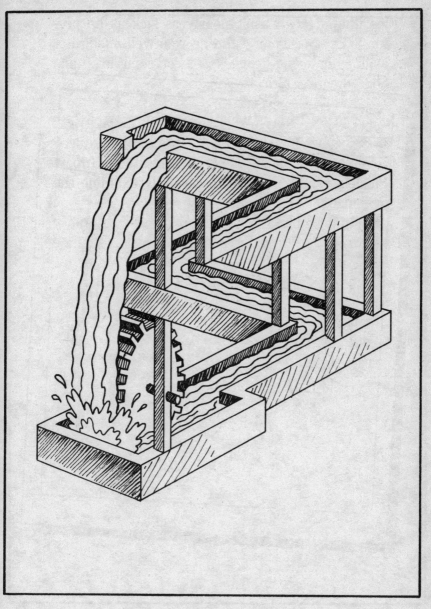

EXHIBIT B

EXHIBIT C

VERDICT

HUBERT PICKLE FAKED HIS DISABILITY.

Pickle claimed that he barely could get out of bed to open the door. He had to brace himself on the chair.

In **EXHIBIT B**, the corner of the bedsheet is turned down on the side nearest the fireplace. If Pickle had been in bed when the investigator knocked, he would have gotten out on the side by the door.

Pickle had been out of bed when the investigator arrived. He had started the fire. Pickle pretended to be sicker than he really was.

The Case of the
Red Balloons

LADIES AND GENTLEMEN OF THE JURY:
A person who helps someone commit a crime
is called an *accessory*. If he or she is found guilty,
an accessory can be punished by the court.

The town of Clemens, represented by the district attorney, accuses Woody Baker of being an
accessory in operating a dishonest game at the
Clemens Carnival. People who played the game
were cheated out of their money.

Mr. Baker, the defendant, says he never was
near the faked game and is being wrongly accused
of the crime.

The Clemens Carnival is the town's major event
of the year. It features top-name entertainment
and has rides, sideshows, and games of skill and
chance.

At this year's carnival, one game drew very
large crowds. It had thirty balloons of different
colors. The game operator, later identified as Otto
Merrell, held the balloon strings. Players paid
$1.00 to pick a string from the tangled ends that
hung down below his hand and pull out a balloon.

47

Prizes were awarded if certain balloons were chosen. The big prize was an expensive watch. It went to the person who pulled out one of the red balloons.

Officer Carlton Dempsy of the Clemens Police Department was called to the stand to testify:

"Everyone has a great time at the carnival except for us. The police work extra hard to manage the crowd of people that flow into town.

"The day after the carnival opened, we got a tip that the balloon game was faked. One woman lost more than $20.00 trying to pick the red balloon. All she ever won was a lot of junk.

"I decided to watch the balloon game myself from the rear of the crowd.

"After a few people lost, the crowd started to thin out. Then a man wearing sunglasses stepped up to try his luck. He gave the game operator a dollar and tugged on a string. Out came a red balloon.

"The man became very excited. He kept on shouting and created a big stir. He yelled that he had just won a wristwatch. New crowds of people lined up to play the balloon game."

Officer Dempsy states that the man who won was a "shill." That's carnival talk for a person who is hired by the game operator to make believe it's easy to win. A shill knows how the fake game works and secretly returns the prize at the end of the day.

Officer Dempsy continued his testimony:

"I kept watching the balloon game after the man with the sunglasses won. Then I pushed through the crowd and headed for the game operator, Otto Merrell. I wanted to take a look at the balloon strings he was holding.

"Merrell saw me coming, grabbed his money, and ran down the midway. He was out of sight before I could catch him."

The district attorney presented EXHIBIT A, which shows how the balloon game is usually faked. The strings tied to the red balloons are folded back and hidden in the game operator's hand. People who play the game never get a chance to pull them.

A short time later, as Officer Dempsy was walking around the carnival grounds, he saw a man who resembled the shill. Although the man was not wearing sunglasses, he looked just like the person who had pulled out the red balloon.

The man was arrested as an accessory to a dishonest carnival game.

The man gave his name as Woody Baker and Hobart Gap as his home town.

The district attorney showed EXHIBIT B, the application form that Otto Merrell filled out when he applied for permission to run the carnival game. Woody Baker came from the same town as Otto Merrell.

Woody Baker took the stand in his own defense.

He claims he is innocent. The policeman made a big mistake.

I quote from his testimony. First the question and then his answer:

Q: Did you know the carnival operator, Otto Merrell?

A: Sure I know him. We come from the same town. He was a shady character. But I haven't seen him for years.

Q: What were you doing in Clemens?

A: The same as everyone else. I went to the carnival. I go every year.

Q: Did you play the balloon game?

A: I never went near any of the games. I just got there and went directly to see my favorite sideshow, the Daredevil Motorcycles.

Q: Is there anyone who saw you at the sideshow?

A: Listen. I don't live in Clemens. I was only visiting. The people at the sideshow were all strangers to me.

Woody Baker says Officer Dempsy has mistaken him for the shill. He asks the court to study the policeman's notebook, which is entered as EXHIBIT C.

"Even his notes say I wasn't wearing sunglasses. The man at the balloon game was. How could he say I looked like that man? Some people are hard to describe when they wear sunglasses."

Woody Baker claims his arrest is a case of mistaken identity. He says he was not involved in the fake carnival game.

LADIES AND GENTLEMEN OF THE JURY:
You have just heard the Case of the Red Balloons. You must decide the merits of the town's accusation. Be sure to carefully examine the evidence in EXHIBITS A, B, and C.

Was Woody Baker involved as an accessory to the dishonest balloon game? Or was the policeman mistaken?

EXHIBIT A

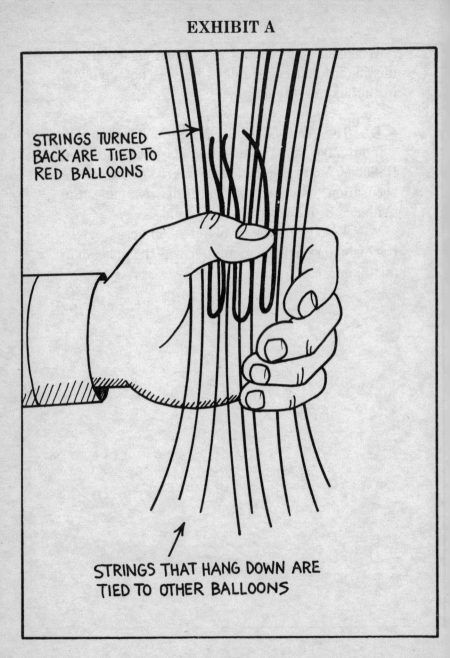

STRINGS TURNED BACK ARE TIED TO RED BALLOONS

STRINGS THAT HANG DOWN ARE TIED TO OTHER BALLOONS

EXHIBIT B

APPLICATION
CARNIVAL BOOTH

NAME: OTTO MERRELL

ADDRESS: 166 FRONT ST.
HOBART GAP, TX.

NATURE OF BOOTH: STRING GAME.
PICK A STRING ATTACHED TO COLORED
BALLOONS. PRIZES GIVEN FOR THE
COLOR BALLOON CHOSEN

IS BOOTH A GAME OF SKILL? NO

SIZE OF BOOTH: 10 FT. X 18 FT.

ELECTRICITY REQUIRED: NO

Otto Merrell
SIGNATURE

EXHIBIT C

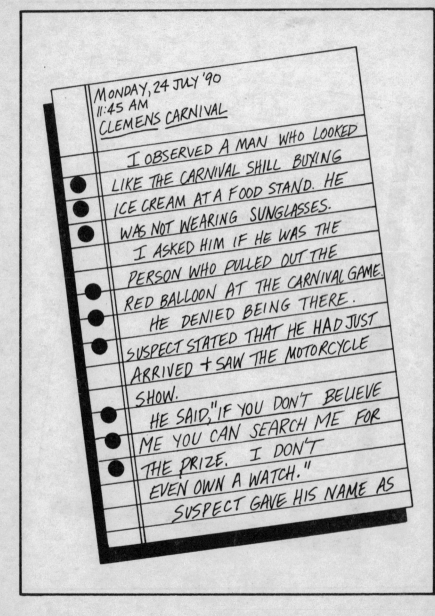

MONDAY, 24 JULY '90
11:45 AM
CLEMENS CARNIVAL

    I OBSERVED A MAN WHO LOOKED LIKE THE CARNIVAL SHILL BUYING ICE CREAM AT A FOOD STAND. HE WAS NOT WEARING SUNGLASSES.
    I ASKED HIM IF HE WAS THE PERSON WHO PULLED OUT THE RED BALLOON AT THE CARNIVAL GAME. HE DENIED BEING THERE. SUSPECT STATED THAT HE HAD JUST ARRIVED + SAW THE MOTORCYCLE SHOW.
    HE SAID, "IF YOU DON'T BELIEVE ME YOU CAN SEARCH ME FOR THE PRIZE. I DON'T EVEN OWN A WATCH."
    SUSPECT GAVE HIS NAME AS

VERDICT

WOODY BAKER WAS AN ACCESSORY.

In the policeman's notebook of EXHIBIT C, Baker was asked if he was the person who pulled out the red balloon.

In his reply, Baker claimed he never was near the balloon game. He offered to be searched and told the policeman he didn't even own a watch.

But Baker could not have known that a wristwatch was the prize unless he had been at the fake carnival game.

The Case of the Confusing Candy

LADIES AND GENTLEMEN OF THE JURY:
It is against the law to sell a product that purposely can be confused with someone else's. This can happen when one company calls its product by the same name that is already used by another company.

To do so is called *unfair trade practice*.

Bodine Candy Company is suing Marjorie Bodine for selling chocolates under the Bodine name. Ms. Bodine, the defendant, claims her father sold Bodine Chocolates long before Bodine Candy Company ever existed. She says that he was the first to use the Bodine name.

Alfred Pullman, who is president of Bodine Candy Company, has testified as follows:

"I became the president of our company three years ago after our founder, Harold Bodine, retired. We make the chewiest chewing gum in the country.

"Oh, excuse me while I take this gum out of my mouth.

"Our company started in 1975, when Harold Bodine made an important discovery in his kitchen. By mixing together some secret ingredients, he could make a gum that crackled and sparkled when you chewed it.

"If you chewed it in the dark, every time your mouth opened, tiny sparks flew out.

"Harold Bodine called it 'Bodine Chewing Gum' and began selling it through local stores. The gum became popular immediately. Kids kept on asking for Bodine gum.

"Soon demand for the gum spread to neighboring towns. Then orders started rolling in from outside the state. Today the Bodine Candy Company has three plants and warehouses all over the country."

Mr. Pullman continued his testimony:

"Our gum was so popular that we came out with candy corn, coconut bars, licorice, and other candies, all with the Bodine name."

EXHIBIT A is a box of Bodine Jewel Berry Drops. The name is prominently displayed.

"You've heard our slogan, 'Throw in a Bodine and throw out your worries.' Our gum and candies are so delicious, they make people happy."

Bodine Candy Company accuses Marjorie Bodine of using the Bodine name because the company made it famous. The company believes she made up the story about her father selling chocolates before Bodine Candy Company was formed.

The company asks the court to stop her from selling her chocolates in the state. It wants her to change the name because people will confuse it with Bodine products.

As proof of the confusion they enter, as EXHIBIT B, a box of Bodine Chocolates sold by Marjorie Bodine.

The defendant, Ms. Bodine, claims that she has the right to use the name Bodine. She says that the chocolate recipe was her grandmother's. Her grandmother had left school after the third grade to make chocolates in their family's candy shop in France.

When Marjorie's father, Philip, moved to the United States, he brought boxes of her grandmother's chocolates with him. That was more than twenty years ago. It was five years before Harold Bodine discovered his chewing gum.

Marjorie's father was a door-to-door brush salesman. He decided to make extra money by selling Grandma Bodine's chocolates to his customers. Grandma Bodine sent boxes of her candy to Philip from her shop in France.

Last year, Marjorie Bodine decided to quit her job and sell chocolate candy using her grandmother's recipe. She never knew her grandmother, but found the candy recipe among her father's letters.

Lawyers for the defense called to the stand

Gretchen Potts, who was one of Philip Bodine's customers.

We quote from her testimony. First the question and then her answer:

Q: Did you ever buy anything from Philip Bodine?

A: Oh my, yes. He had the fuzziest brushes. Philip was such a nice man. He didn't speak English very well, but he had the cutest accent.

Q: What else did you buy from him?

A: Oh, you mean the chocolates? Yes, he sold the most delicious chocolate candy.

Q: When you bought the chocolates from Philip Bodine, how were they packaged? Were they in a Bodine Chocolate box?

A: I really can't remember. He always made up a special order for me. Every time he came by to sell me his brushes, I would give him my large silver candy dish. He would return it the next day filled with his delicious chocolates.

Q: Did you ever see the original box of chocolates that he used to fill your silver candy dish? Was it from a candy box that had "Bodine Chocolates" printed on it?

A: Oh, I have such a terrible memory. But I seem to recall that he showed me a candy box one day. I think he said it came from his mother's candy shop.

EXHIBIT C is Marjorie Bodine's chocolate recipe that her grandmother sent to her father.

Marjorie Bodine says she has every right to use the Bodine name on her chocolate candy. Her father used the Bodine name first, years before people ever heard of Bodine Candy Company.

LADIES AND GENTLEMEN OF THE JURY:

You have just heard the Case of the Confusing Candy. You must decide the merits of Bodine Candy Company's claim. Be sure to carefully examine the evidence in EXHIBITS A, B, and C.

Should Marjorie Bodine be allowed to sell Bodine Chocolates? Or did she make up the story about her grandmother's candy?

EXHIBIT C

October 5

Dear Philip,

Here is my recipe for my cocoa cones:

Sift one cup sugar
Whip until stiff —
    3 egg whites
    pinch of salt

Slowly mix sugar into the whip.
    Then add:
    2 teaspoons water
    1 teaspoon vanilla

Whip for 5 minutes and add:
    3 tablespoons cocoa

Drop the batter from a spoon into
tin. Shape the candy into small cones
Bake until a little dry.

I hope you like my candy recipe.
Do not eat too many at one time.

Love
Momma

VERDICT

MARJORIE MADE UP THE STORY ABOUT THE CANDY.

Marjorie claimed her grandmother left school after the third grade to work in the family candy shop in France. And the witness said that her father, Philip, spoke poor English.

The recipe in EXHIBIT C is a fake, written by Marjorie Bodine. If it had been from her grandmother, the recipe would not be in English. It would have been written in French.

The Case of the Dangerous Dog

LADIES AND GENTLEMEN OF THE JURY:

If a dog bites someone and causes serious injury, the owner is responsible. But if the person bitten was being cruel to the animal, that may be a different matter.

Consider this point of law as you hear the case before you today.

Andy Porter, the plaintiff, is suing for injuries he received when Rita Finch's dog attacked him.

Mrs. Finch, the defendant, claims that her dog is harmless. It bit Andy because he hit the dog with a big stick.

The plaintiff explained to the court how his injury happened:

"My name is Andy Porter. I'm a ninth-grader at Eagle Rock High School. Every morning before class, I deliver newspapers to the people in the Glen Cove section of town. One of the houses is 28 Glen Cove Lane. That's where Mrs. Finch lives.

"About a week before I was bitten, Mrs. Finch

began letting Piper out to play on the front lawn. Piper is a large bulldog.

"Every morning when I delivered the newspaper, the dog would start snarling at me. He had a terrible bark. It was frightening.

"I had to deliver the newspapers to keep my job. So I figured it was safer to throw the paper on Mrs. Finch's lawn and run. I didn't want to get too close to Piper."

On the morning of October 16, when Andy Porter was delivering to the Finch house, Andy claims Piper attacked him. The dog leaped at Andy, biting him on his right arm.

Andy Porter's arm was covered with blood. He flagged down a passing car and was driven to the hospital emergency room. The wound required ten stitches.

When the boy returned home from the hospital, his mother took a photograph of the injury. This is entered as EXHIBIT A.

Andy Porter is suing Piper's owner for medical expenses and his pain and suffering because of the injury.

Andy missed three days of school. He even gave up his delivery route.

The plaintiff continued his testimony:

"When Mrs. Finch began letting Piper out, I phoned her and said I was scared he might bite me. She just laughed. She said I was a sissy, and that I didn't have to be afraid of Piper."

EXHIBIT B is a photograph of the shirt Andy was wearing. It shows more details of the attack. The dog bit through the shirt, making a bloody tear. Andy insists he did nothing to provoke the attack.

In Rita Finch's testimony to the court, she tells a different story. She admits that her dog bit the plaintiff. But she says Piper is harmless. He attacks only when he has a reason.

I will quote from Mrs. Finch's testimony. First the question and then her answer:

Q: Has your dog ever bitten a person before?

A: No, never. He's very well trained. Why, I even gave him lessons at the Ruff Ruff and Tuff Doggie School.

Q: If a burglar broke into your house, do you think Piper would attack?

A: Of course! My dog isn't that timid. The school taught Piper how to be a good watchdog.

Q: Did you see the attack against Andy Porter?

A: Sure I did. But he made my dog do it. The boy swung at Piper with a big stick. Piper was only protecting himself.

Q: How do you know?

A: I had let Piper out on the front lawn and was making breakfast. All of a sudden I heard him barking real loud. Then I heard a whine, like he was hurt. I looked out the window and there was Andy Porter.

Q: What was he doing?

A: I saw him pushing Piper with a big stick. I was horrified. All of a sudden, Andy raised the stick high over his head and struck at Piper. My dog dodged the swing and the stick glanced off Piper's tail.

Q: Did you actually see your dog bite the plaintiff?

A: Yes, I saw it all happen. I dashed out the front door as fast as I could. Andy had raised the stick high over his head for another strike. That's when Piper jumped up and bit him.

Q: Andy Porter claims that he never hit Piper. Is there any question in your mind that your dog was protecting himself?

A: The boy is flat out lying. He just doesn't like dogs. Andy told me so over the telephone. He hit Piper because he was afraid of him.

The defense entered as evidence EXHIBIT C. It is the stick Mrs. Finch says Andy Porter was holding. When Piper bit him, the boy dropped it and ran.

Mrs. Finch says the charges against her should be dismissed. Piper attacked Andy because the boy hit him.

LADIES AND GENTLEMEN OF THE JURY: You have just heard the Case of the Dangerous

Dog. You must decide the merits of Andy Porter's claim. Be sure to carefully examine the evidence in EXHIBITS A, B, and C.

Did Andy Porter strike Mrs. Finch's dog? Or did the dog attack him without cause?

EXHIBIT C

VERDICT

ANDY PORTER STRUCK THE DOG.

Piper's bite went through Andy's sleeve and into his arm.

In EXHIBIT A, the dog's bite mark is on the *upper* part of Andy's arm. But the tear in his shirt, in EXHIBIT B, is on the *lower* part of the sleeve.

This could happen only if Andy's arm was raised. Then the lower part of his sleeve would *slide down* his raised arm.

Rita Finch had told the truth. Andy held the stick high over his head to strike her dog. Piper bit him while Andy's arm was in the air.

The Case of the Big Bank Robbery

LADIES AND GENTLEMEN OF THE JURY:

To find a person guilty of a crime, you must have sufficient proof that he or she did it.

Keep this in mind as you go over the facts in this case. Since we are in criminal court today, the State is the accuser.

The State, represented by the district attorney, has accused Bret Brewster of robbery. The State believes he is one of two men who held up an armored truck. Police have been unable to locate the other man.

Mr. Brewster, the defendant, has pleaded not guilty and claims his arrest is a mistake.

On the morning of February 16, as the guard for Grinks Protection Service delivered money to Fidelity Bank, he was held up by a masked man.

Edgar Holmes, the guard, described for the court what happened:

"I had just pulled into the bank parking lot. I go there every morning, just before it opens.

"I had put on the brakes and unlocked the truck door. Suddenly the door swung wide open. I found myself staring at the barrel of a long revolver.

"The man pointing it at me was wearing a mask. He told me that if I cooperated, I wouldn't get hurt.

"The robber ordered me to open the back of my truck and hand over the money bags inside."

Edgar Holmes followed the masked man's instructions. The robber handed the bags to a second man who was waiting in a nearby car. Then he jumped in and the two men sped away.

The guard provided police with a description of the robbers:

"The man with the gun was tall — maybe six feet. He was wearing a gray sweater and chinos. The man in the car wore a mask, too. I could see he had a beard."

The robber left a telling clue. When police checked the truck's door handle, they found a set of fingerprints. The prints were identified as those of Frank Paxton, a man with a previous criminal record.

Paxton is the owner of Frank's Pizzeria. After getting a search warrant, police hurried to the pizza store only to find it was closed. A sign was hanging on the front door.

A photograph of the pizza store is entered as EXHIBIT A.

When police knocked on the door, a man opened it. He was eating a baloney sandwich. The man identified himself as Bret Brewster. He was of short, heavy build and had a beard. The owner of the store was nowhere to be found.

Police guarded Bret Brewster as they searched the store. Inside two empty pizza boxes, they found all of the stolen bank money, neatly stacked in packets of crisp hundred-dollar bills.

Brewster was placed under arrest and charged as the bearded man driving the getaway car. Police believe that Bret Brewster had returned to the store and planned to pick up his share of the robbery money.

The police searched Brewster. His wallet contained $73.00. He also had a key to Frank's Pizzeria.

This key is entered as EXHIBIT B.

The State asked Brewster about his association with Frank Paxton:

Q: Is it true that you and Frank Paxton palled around together?

A: Sure, we used to be friends. But for the past year I haven't seen much of him.

Q: Then what were you doing in his store?

A: This sounds strange, but you've got to believe me. I hadn't seen or heard from Frank in months. Then, one day, he phoned long distance and asked for a favor.

Q: Where did he phone from?

A: That's just it. Frank wouldn't say. He just

told me he had to be out of town for a few weeks. He asked me to go over to his pizza store and put out the garbage and check that the oven was shut off. He told me to hang up a CLOSED sign.

Q: How did you get into his store?

A: When he phoned, Frank told me I could pick up his key. He said that he had mailed it to the store, and I would find it when I got there.

Bret Brewster claims the key the police found in his possession belonged to Frank Paxton. Brewster never had one. He went inside the store only to do Paxton a favor.

The defense claims the State does not have sufficient proof that Brewster was a partner to the robbery. The only fingerprints on the pizza boxes were those of Frank Paxton.

This fingerprint report is entered as EXHIBIT C.

The defense argues that the guard's description of the man in the car was not detailed. Hundreds of men in the town have beards.

Bret Brewster's lawyer claims he is innocent. He asks that the charges be dismissed.

LADIES AND GENTLEMEN OF THE JURY:
You have just heard the Case of the Big Bank Robbery. You must decide the merits of the

State's accusation. Be sure to carefully examine the evidence in EXHIBITS A, B, and C.

Was Bret Brewster involved in the holdup? Or did someone else help Frank Paxton steal the bank money?

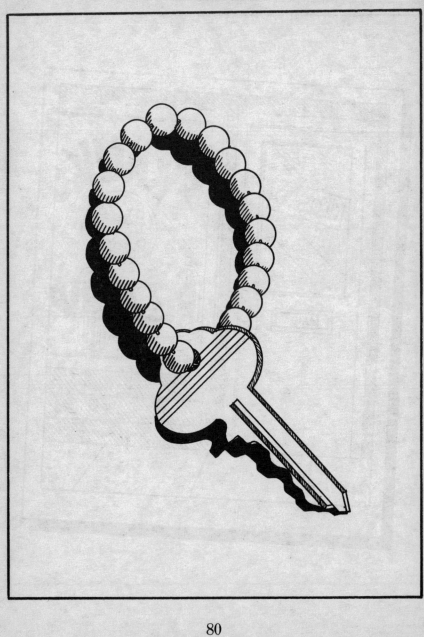

EXHIBIT C

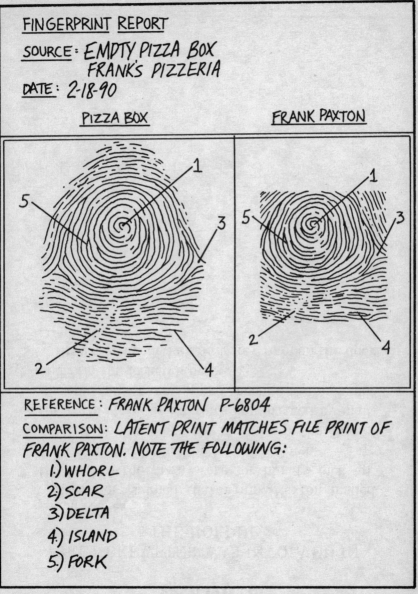

FINGERPRINT REPORT

SOURCE: EMPTY PIZZA BOX
         FRANK'S PIZZERIA

DATE: 2-18-90

PIZZA BOX   FRANK PAXTON

REFERENCE: FRANK PAXTON P-6804

COMPARISON: LATENT PRINT MATCHES FILE PRINT OF
FRANK PAXTON. NOTE THE FOLLOWING:
1.) WHORL
2.) SCAR
3.) DELTA
4.) ISLAND
5.) FORK

VERDICT

BRET BREWSTER WAS INVOLVED IN THE HOLDUP.

Brewster claimed that Frank Paxton mailed the key to the pizza store for him to pick up. Brewster said he had no key of his own.

EXHIBIT A shows the mail slot in the door of the pizza store. If Paxton's key arrived by mail, it would have been slipped through the mail slot and *into* the locked store.

Brewster needed *another* key to open the door — his own.

The Case of the Thirsty Helper

LADIES AND GENTLEMEN OF THE JURY:

When a person is hired to work by the hour, she or he is expected to do the job responsibly. Otherwise, the employer does not have to pay in full.

Consider this as you listen to both sides of the case presented to you today.

Donald Breen, the plaintiff, says he overpaid a woman he hired to work for him. She only did half as much work as she should have. But Emily Chowder, the defendant, disagrees.

Mr. Breen recently purchased an old motel located on a main highway. He fixed up the rooms so they looked brand new. A week before the motel opened, Breen planned to send out announcements.

Mr. Breen hired Emily Chowder to help with the mailing. Her job was to take 1,000 announcements, fold and stuff them into envelopes, and paste on stamps.

The two agreed that Emily would be paid $6.00 an hour for the job.

The plaintiff explained to the court why he is suing Emily Chowder:

"It was about eight o'clock in the morning when Miss Chowder arrived at my motel office. She was ready to start the job. I left her alone at the desk while I ran some errands.

"When I got back later that afternoon, Miss Chowder was still at the desk, folding the letters and stuffing them in envelopes. She had finished only half the job.

"The woman said she had been working for eight hours straight. I was surprised she hadn't finished. But I paid her for the eight hours anyway and said I would finish the rest of the job myself."

EXHIBIT A is a photo of Emily Chowder at the desk when Donald Breen returned. Notice the piles of announcements that still need to be stuffed into envelopes.

Mr. Breen continued his testimony.

"I couldn't understand what took her so long until I noticed that the rear door to the office was open. It leads to my motel's swimming pool.

"Suddenly I realized why Miss Chowder had finished only half the job. There, by the edge of the pool, I saw puddles of water.

"Emily Chowder wasn't just stuffing envelopes all day. She did some goofing off, diving and

84

swimming in the pool. The fresh puddles of water prove it."

EXHIBIT B is a photograph of the deep end of the pool where Donald Breen saw the puddles.

Breen was very upset. He timed himself while he stuffed the remaining 500 envelopes. He finished the job in four hours. It had taken Emily eight hours to do the first 500 envelopes.

Mr. Breen is suing to recover the extra money he paid her. He says he should pay the woman only for four hours of work.

Emily Chowder took the stand and described her work to the court. She insisted it really took her the full eight hours.

"I'm a very particular person, you know. I figured Mr. Breen wanted me to do a very neat job, so I was very careful. I neatly folded each announcement before I inserted it.

"Mr. Breen didn't even have a moistener for me. I had to lick the envelopes with my tongue. That took extra time. And the glue tasted just terrible."

Emily Chowder explained to the court why she feels that Breen is mistaken. First the question and then her answer:

Q: Why did Mr. Breen finish the job much faster than you?
A: I think he was trying to prove I was too slow

so he could get some of his money back. I could have done the job a lot faster, too. But it wouldn't have been very neat.

Q: Did you take any time off during the eight hours?

A: No, I didn't even eat lunch. I worked straight through without stopping.

Q: Then how do you account for the puddles around the pool?

A: It's all because I had to lick those envelopes shut. I stopped each time I got real thirsty. My tongue and throat became very dry.

Miss Chowder claimed that she looked around for a water fountain, but couldn't find one. Then she went outside by the pool and found a hose.

Miss Chowder turned on the water several times during the day to drink from the hose. But the last time, just before Mr. Breen returned, she had an accident.

"As I was drinking from the hose, Mr. Breen's dog came running toward me. It knocked the hose right out of my hand. The water sprayed everywhere.

"The water came out so fast that the hose kept on whipping back and forth. When I turned off the water, the whole area was drenched."

The defendant offered as evidence EXHIBIT C. It shows the hose she drank from which was near the motel pool.

Emily Chowder claims that she never swam in Donald Breen's pool. She worked nonstop, except when she got thirsty. She says she is entitled to keep all the money for her eight hours of work.

LADIES AND GENTLEMEN OF THE JURY:
You have just heard the Case of the Thirsty Helper. You must decide the merits of Donald Breen's claim. Be sure to carefully examine the evidence in EXHIBITS A, B, and C.

Did Emily Chowder do a full eight hours work? Or did she take time off to go swimming?

EXHIBIT A

EXHIBIT C

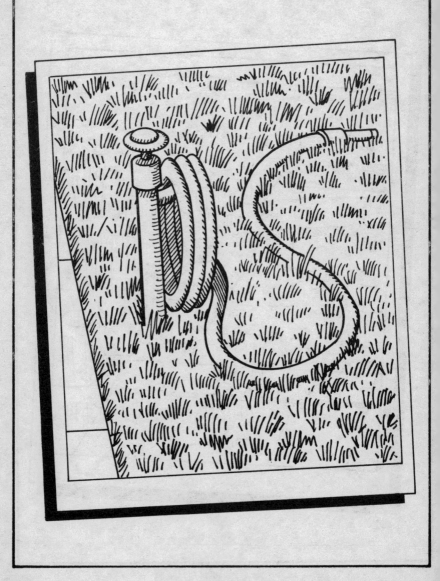

VERDICT

EMILY CHOWDER NEVER WENT INTO
THE POOL.

Had Emily swam in the pool, her hair would
have been soaked, too. She couldn't possibly have
had the neatly styled hair shown in EXHIBIT A.